A Note From Rick Renner

I am on a personal quest to see a "revival of the Bible" so people can establish their lives on a firm foundation that will stand strong and endure the test as end-time storm winds begin to intensify.

In order to experience a revival of the Bible in your personal life, it is important to take time each day to read, receive, and apply its truths to your life. James tells us that if we will continue in the perfect law of liberty — refusing to be forgetful hearers, but determined to be doers — we will be blessed in our ways. As you watch or listen to the programs in this series and work through this corresponding study guide, I trust you will search the Scriptures and allow the Holy Spirit to help you hear something new from God's Word that applies specifically to your life. I encourage you to be a doer of the Word He reveals to you. Whatever the cost, I assure you — it will be worth it.

> Thy words were found, and I did eat them;
> and thy word was unto me the joy and rejoicing of mine heart:
> for I am called by thy name, O Lord God of hosts.
> — Jeremiah 15:16

Your brother and friend in Jesus Christ,

Rick Renner

Unless otherwise indicated, all scripture quotations are taken from the *King James Version* of the Bible.

Scripture quotations marked (*NKJV*) are taken from the *New King James Version*®. Copyright © 1982 by Thomas Nelson. Used by permission. All rights reserved.

Scripture quotations marked *RIV* are taken from *Renner Interpretive Version*. Copyright © 2021 by Rick Renner.

How To Heal the Sick

Copyright © 2023 by Rick Renner
1814 W. Tacoma St.
Broken Arrow, OK 74012-1406

Published by Rick Renner Ministries
www.renner.org

ISBN 13: 978-1-6675-0360-8

eBook ISBN 13: 978-1-6675-0361-5

All rights reserved. No portion of this book may be reproduced or transmitted in any form or by any means — electronic, mechanical, photocopy, recording, scanning, or other — except for brief quotations in critical reviews or articles, without the prior written permission of the Publisher.

How To Use This Study Guide

This five-lesson study guide corresponds to *"How To Heal the Sick" with Rick Renner* **(Renner TV)**. Each lesson in this study guide covers a topic that is addressed during the program series, with questions and references supplied to draw you deeper into your own private study of the Scriptures on this subject.

To derive the most benefit from this study guide, consider the following:

First, watch or listen to the program prior to working through the corresponding lesson in this guide. (Programs can also be viewed at **renner.org** by clicking on the Media/Archives links or on our Renner Ministries YouTube channel.)

Second, take the time to look up the scriptures included in each lesson. Prayerfully consider their application to your own life.

Third, use a journal or notebook to make note of your answers to each lesson's Study Questions and Practical Application challenges.

Fourth, invest specific time in prayer and in the Word of God to consult with the Holy Spirit. Write down the scriptures or insights He reveals to you.

Finally, take action! Whatever the Lord tells you to do according to His Word, do it.

For added insights on this subject, it is recommended that you obtain *Bodily Healing and the Atonement* by Dr. T. J. McCrossan and *The Grace of Healing* by Bob Yandian. You may also select from Rick's other available resources by placing your order at **renner.org** or by calling 1-800-742-5593.

TOPIC
The Types of Sicknesses Jesus Healed

SCRIPTURES

1. **Hebrews 13:8** — Jesus Christ the same yesterday, and to day, and for ever.

2. **John 21:25** — And there are also many other things which Jesus did, the which, if they should be written every one, I suppose that even the world itself could not contain the books that should be written. Amen.

3. **Matthew 4:23-25** — And Jesus went about all Galilee, teaching in their synagogues, and preaching the gospel of the kingdom, and healing all manner of sickness and all manner of disease among the people. And his fame went throughout all Syria: and they brought unto him all sick people that were taken with divers diseases and torments, and those which were possessed with devils, and those which were lunatick, and those that had the palsy; and he healed them. And there followed him great multitudes of people from Galilee, and from Decapolis, and from Jerusalem, and from Judaea, and from beyond Jordan.

GREEK WORDS

1. "healing" — **ἰάομαι** (*iaomai*): to cure; to be doctored; pictures healing power that progressively reverses a condition; denotes progressive, restorative healing power

2. "healing" — **θεραπεύω** (*therapeuo*): therapy; pictures a healing touch that requires corresponding actions

3. "sickness" — **νόσος** (*nosos*): a terminal condition for which there is no natural cure; in the ancient world, it denoted a sickness that was the result of evil spirits; a condition for which there was no known cure

4. "disease" — **μαλακία** (*malakia*): a crippling or debilitating form of sickness

5. "fame" — **ἀκοή** (*akoe*): pictures the ear; denotes ears filled with information; hence, rumors or stories

6. "brought" — **προσφέρω** (*prospheros*): to physically carry, likely because they were too sick to walk

7. "sick" — **κακῶς** (*kakos*): sick in a bad, foul way; often associated with demonic activity

8. "divers" — **ποικίλος** (*poikilos*): assorted, divers, multiple, or various; same word used in the Septuagint to describe Joseph's coat of many colors

9. "diseases" — **νόσος** (*nosos*): a terminal condition for which there is no natural cure; in the ancient world, it denoted a sickness that was the result of evil spirits; a condition for which there was no known cure

10. "oppressing torments" — **βασάνοις συνεχομένους** (*basanois sunechomenous*): one who is oppressed or tormented

11. "possessed with devils" — **δαιμονίζομαι** (*daimonidzomai*): those who were demonized

12. "lunatick" — **σεληνιάζομαι** (*seleniadzomai*): moonstruck; an event that happened during the full moon; a sickness resulting from dabbling in the occult

13. "palsy" — **παραλυτικός** (*paralutikos*): those who were paralyzed

14. "healed" — **θεραπεύω** (*therapeuo*): therapy; pictures a healing touch that requires corresponding actions

SYNOPSIS

The five lessons in this study titled ***How To Heal the Sick*** will focus on the following topics:

- The Types of Sicknesses Jesus Healed

- The Methods Jesus Used To Heal the Sick

- Examples of 'Therapy' in the Healing Ministry of Jesus

- Other Insights Into Healing

- Healing Is in Your Hands

The emphasis of this lesson:

There are two main types of healing that Jesus did: one was gradual and the other was a therapeutic restoration that required corresponding actions from the person being healed. Jesus healed people of terminal

illnesses as well as crippling and debilitating conditions. He was never in a rush, but took His time to minister to each person.

As we begin this series, it's interesting to know how it came about. Pulling from the pages of his life, Rick shares how many years ago when he and Denise first began their teaching ministry in 1985, they traveled with their sons to churches all over the United States. When it came time to pray with people at the conclusion of each service, Rick and Denise would lay hands on the sick and believe in faith for their healing. Sometimes they saw great results, and other times the results were very disappointing.

Why are some healed and some are not? Rick began to wonder. The disparity in the outcome drove him to dig deep into the gospels and study every instance of healing and miracles recorded there. As he went verse by verse through Matthew, Mark, Luke and John, he began to discover treasures that no one had ever taught him before, and that is what he unpacks in these 5 lessons.

Jesus' Life Was Jampacked With Activity

First, it is vital that we realize God does not change, and neither does Jesus. Hebrews 13:8 declares, "Jesus Christ the same yesterday, and to day, and for ever." This is a truth we need to settle in our heart and mind. If Jesus healed *then*, He is still healing *now*, and He's going to heal tomorrow. The Jesus who is alive today is no different than the One who walked the earth in New Testament times.

The apostle John makes an amazing statement at the very end of his gospel. He says, "And there are also many other things which Jesus did, the which, if they should be written every one, I suppose that even the world itself could not contain the books that should be written. Amen" (John 21:25).

If we were to chronologically put together all the days of Jesus' life that are recorded in the four gospels — from His birth to His resurrection all the way to the moment He ascended into Heaven — how many days do you think we have a record of? Although you may think it's three and half years, that is not the case. Yes, what is recorded covers the span of Jesus' three-and-a-half-year ministry, but the actual number of documented days within that time period is estimated by scholars to be somewhere between 23 and 52 days of Jesus life.

The truth is, we only have a few snap shots of what He did. Can you imagine how much text and how many books we would have if EVERY detail of what Jesus did throughout His entire earthly ministry would have been written down? That's why John said, "…I suppose that even the world itself could not contain the books that should be written. Amen" (John 21:25). Interestingly, when you read this in Greek, it would be better translated, "I suppose, of course it's not possible, but if it were possible, I suppose that even the world itself could not contain the books that should be written." This tells us that if we had been walking with Jesus during His time on earth, there would have always been some manifestation of His power to see and hear.

There Are Two Main Types of Healing Mentioned in the Gospels

In the four gospels, there are two primary words used to describe the healing ministry of Jesus. The first one is the Greek word *iaomai*, which means *to cure* or *to be doctored*. It pictures *healing power that progressively reverses a condition*. It denotes *progressive, restorative healing power to cure* and carries the idea of *being doctored*. Additionally, it describes *a healing power that progressively reverses a condition*. It is just as good as any kind of healing power, but it is not instantaneous. Instead, it is gradual and works over a period of time, progressively reversing a condition.

The second word used to describe the healing ministry of Jesus is the one most often used in the gospels. It is the Greek word *therapeuo*, and it's where we get the word *therapy* from. It pictures *a healing touch that requires corresponding actions*. In other words, this healing results not just from the efforts of the person praying, but also from the actions of the individual being prayed for. Some kind of corresponding action was required in order for the person to experience healing.

If you think about it, a therapist doesn't do the restorative work by himself. The person he's working with must cooperate. That is the inherent meaning of this Greek word *therapeuo*, the primary word used to describe the healing ministry of Jesus. Matthew 4:23 is a perfect example. Here, Matthew writes, "And Jesus went about all Galilee, teaching in their synagogues, and preaching the gospel of the kingdom, and healing all manner of sickness and all manner of disease among the people."

The word "healing" in this verse is *therapeuo*, the word for *therapy*. As Jesus was praying for people and ministering to their needs, He wasn't doing all the action by Himself. Each person cooperated with Jesus in the therapeutic process. After He touched them and prayed for them, He asked them to do something in faith to help bring about their healing.

This means Jesus took a great deal of time with each person, and it reveals a major reason so many of us don't see more healing results when we pray for people today. Sadly, we are too often in a hurry to get to the next person and the person after that. Jesus wasn't in a hurry. For example, He stopped and said to the person with a withered hand, "…Stretch forth thine hand. And he stretched it forth; and it was restored whole, like as the other" (Matthew 12:13).

If you think about it, it would have been very difficult for a person with a withered hand to stretch it out, but that was the corresponding action Jesus required of him. As he worked with Jesus, Jesus' healing power was released. We might say Jesus was *therapying* this man — that's a literal translation of the word *therapeuo*. He required people to do something they couldn't do previously, and as a result of their obedient cooperation, He healed all manner of sickness and disease among them.

Jesus Healed the Terminally Ill
as Well as the Weak and Crippled

Looking once more at Matthew 4:23, it says, "And Jesus went about all Galilee, teaching in their synagogues, and preaching the gospel of the kingdom, and healing all manner of sickness and all manner of disease among the people." Notice it says *sickness* and *disease*. On the surface, these two words my seem to be the same, but they aren't. The word "sickness" here is the Greek word *nosos*, and it describes *a terminal condition for which there is no natural cure*. In the ancient world, it denoted a sickness that was the result of evil spirits. In other words, it was a condition for which there was no known cure.

In contrast, the word "disease" is the Greek word *malakia*, which denotes *a crippling or debilitating form of sickness*. This described a disease that would affect your muscles or your nerves. A person could have this condition and live, but they couldn't function because they were somehow affected by this *malakia* — a crippling or debilitating kind of disease. Amazingly, the Bible says Jesus healed both categories of these sicknesses and diseases.

When we come to Matthew 4:24, it says, "And his fame went throughout all Syria: and they brought unto him all sick people that were taken with divers diseases and torments, and those which were possessed with devils, and those which were lunatick, and those that had the palsy; and he healed them."

First, note the word "fame." It's the Greek word *akoe*, which pictures *the human ear*, but here it denotes *ears filled with information*. Hence, in this verse it pictures people's ears that are buzzing with rumors or stories about the healing ministry of Jesus. As a result of all the stories that were circulating about Jesus, people "…brought unto him [Jesus] all sick people…." (Matthew 4:24).

The word "brought" is a translation of the Greek word *prospheros*, which is a compound of the words *pros*, meaning *toward*, and *phero*, meaning *to carry*. When these words are compounded to form *prospheros*, it means *to physically carry, likely because they were too sick to walk*. Here we find invalids who were so sick they couldn't physically walk to the place where Jesus was ministering. Out of great love, their family and friends picked them up and *prospheros* — they physically carried them to Jesus.

Matthew 4:24 says these people were "sick," which is the Greek word *kakos*. It depicts *someone sick in a bad, foul way*, and this word was often associated with demonic activity. Matthew said these sick people "were taken with divers diseases and torments." The word "divers" is *poikilos* in Greek, and it means *assorted, divers, multiple, or various*. It's the same word used in the Old Testament Greek Septuagint to describe Joseph's coat of many colors. The word "diseases" is, again, the Greek word *nosos*, describing *a terminal condition for which there is no natural cure*. The use of these words indicates that there were many different colors of diseases, but regardless of what assortment it was, Jesus healed every one of them!

Oppression, Depression, and Demonic Possession Were Also Conditions Jesus Healed

Along with these incurable diseases, people were also physically carried to Jesus who suffered with divers "torments." What's interesting is that when you read this in the Greek, it includes a word that doesn't appear in the *King James Version*. The original text says *"oppressing* torments," which depicts *those who were oppressed and were struggling emotionally and mentally with depression*.

Matthew then added that "those which were possessed with devils" were brought to Jesus. The phrase "possessed with devils" is a translation of the Greek word *daimonidzomai*, and it describes *those who were demonized*. It's important to note that a person doesn't have to be fully demon possessed to be demonized. An individual who is demonized can be ill-affected in their minds or somehow be affected in their health by demons. Regardless of the specific struggles these people were facing, Jesus healed them.

Who else did Jesus heal? The Bible says, "…Those which were lunatick, and those that had the palsy; and he healed them" (Matthew 4:24). The word "lunatick" is the Greek word *seleniadzomai*, which means *moonstruck* and depicts *an event that happened during the full moon*. Most likely, it describes a sickness resulting from those who were dabbling in the occult. Because they had opened a door to the realm of darkness, demon spirits began to physically, mentally, and emotionally affect them. In His mercy, Jesus healed these individuals as well.

He also healed those who had "palsy." In Greek, the word "palsy" is *paralutikos*, which describes *those who were paralyzed*. When the Bible says Jesus "healed" those with palsy, the word "healed" is, again, the Greek word *therapeuo*, describing *therapy* and picturing *a healing touch that requires corresponding actions*.

So, when it came to healing the sick, Jesus *therapied* them. Rather than just quickly move them through a prayer line, He stopped and worked with every single person, requiring corresponding actions from them in order for them to experience the healing they desired. He did the praying and released the anointing, but the healing was manifested when the person cooperated with what Jesus asked.

Friend, if you want to see more people healed, you need to do more than just quickly lay your hands on them and whisper a prayer. Like Jesus, you may need to take time to have the person being prayed for do something they couldn't previously do. Having them cooperate in these ways is what the Greek word *therapeuo* means.

STUDY QUESTIONS

Study to shew thyself approved unto God, a workman that needeth not to be ashamed, rightly dividing the word of truth.
— 2 Timothy 2:15

1. The primary New Testament meaning of the word "healing" — the Greek word *therapeuo* — is quite eye-opening. In what ways is this definition different from what you previously understood healing to be?

2. Who can you think of in the Old Testament who cooperated with God to receive their healing? What corresponding actions were they required to do to experience their restoration?

3. Take time to read the story of Naaman and Elisha in Second Kings 5:1-14. What did Elisha instruct Naaman to do to receive his healing? How did Naaman initially react to his instructions? Have you ever responded similarly when God directed you to do something through someone else? What other insights is the Holy Spirit showing you from this passage?

PRACTICAL APPLICATION

**But be ye doers of the word, and not hearers only,
deceiving your own selves.
—James 1:22**

1. What has been your view of God's healing power up to this point? What surprises you most from all that you've heard in this lesson about the various kinds of sicknesses and diseases that Jesus healed?

2. Do you have a desire to see people healed physically, mentally, and emotionally? If so, what is a challenge or disease that weighs on your heart the most? What is something that you would especially like to see someone freed from?

3. Have you seen or heard of someone you know receiving healing from God in the here and now? What amazed you most about their story, and how does it encourage you to believe for your own healing?

TOPIC

The Methods Jesus Used To Heal the Sick

SCRIPTURES

1. **Hebrews 13:8** — Jesus Christ the same yesterday, and to day, and for ever.

2. **John 21:25** — And there are also many other things which Jesus did, the which, if they should be written every one, I suppose that even the world itself could not contain the books that should be written. Amen.

3. **Matthew 4:23-25** — And Jesus went about all Galilee, teaching in their synagogues, and preaching the gospel of the kingdom, and healing all manner of sickness and all manner of disease among the people. And his fame went throughout all Syria: and they brought unto him all sick people that were taken with divers diseases and torments, and those which were possessed with devils, and those which were lunatick, and those that had the palsy; and he healed them. And there followed him great multitudes of people from Galilee, and from Decapolis, and from Jerusalem, and from Judaea, and from beyond Jordan.

4. **Mark 1:32-34** — And at even, when the sun did set, they brought unto him all that were diseased, and them that were possessed with devils. And all the city was gathered together at the door. And he healed many that were sick of divers diseases, and cast out many devils....

5. **Mark 1:39** — And he preached in their synagogues throughout all Galilee, and cast out devils.

6. **Luke 4:40** — Now when the sun was setting, all they that had any sick with divers diseases brought them unto him; and he laid his hands on every one of them, and healed them.

GREEK WORDS

1. "healing" — **θεραπεύω** (*therapeuo*): therapy; pictures a healing touch that requires corresponding actions

2. "sickness" — **νόσος** (*nosos*): a terminal condition for which there is no natural cure; in the ancient world, it denoted a sickness that was the result of evil spirits; a condition for which there was no known cure

3. "disease" — **μαλακία** (*malakia*): a crippling or debilitating form of sickness

4. "fame" — **ἀκοή** (*akoe*): pictures the ear; denotes ears filled with information; hence, rumors or stories

5. "diseases" — **νόσος** (*nosos*): a terminal condition for which there is no natural cure; in the ancient world, it denoted a sickness that was the result of evil spirits; a condition for which there was no known cure

6. "oppressing torments" — **βασάνοις συνεχομένους** (*basanois sunechomenous*): one who is oppressed or tormented

7. "possessed with devils" — **δαιμονίζομαι** (*daimonidzomai*): those who were demonized

8. "lunatick" — **σεληνιάζομαι** (*seleniadzomai*): moonstruck; an event that happened during the full moon; a sickness resulting from dabbling in the occult

9. "palsy" — **παραλυτικός** (*paralutikos*): those who were paralyzed

10. "healed" — **θεραπεύω** (*therapeuo*): therapy; pictures a healing touch that requires corresponding actions

11. "brought" — **φέρω** (*phero*): to physically carry

12. "all" — **πάντας** (*pantas*): absolutely all

13. "diseased" — **ἔχω κακός** (*echo kakos*): miserably afflicted; extremely sick; in the last stage of their condition; a terminal case

14. "many" — **πολύς** (*polus*): many; vast multitudes

15. "sick" — **κακῶς** (*kakos*): sick in a bad, foul way; often associated with demonic activity

16. "divers" — **ποικίλος** (*poikilos*): assorted, diverse, multiple, or various; same word used in the Septuagint to describe Joseph's coat of many colors

17. "cast out" — **ἐκβάλλω** (*ekballo*): to forcibly evict; to cast out

18. "devils" — **δαιμόνιον** (*daimonion*): evil spirits; demons; devils; the ancient world generally believed demons thickly populated the lower

regions of the air and that spirits were the primary cause of disasters and suffering in the earth; this word could depict a person deemed insane; in both secular and New Testament writings, depicted those possessed with evil spirits who suffered spirit-inflicted mental or physical infirmities

19. "sick" — ἀσθένεια (*astheneia*): an all-encompassing term for all types of sickness and disease

20. "every one" — ἕκαστος (*hekastos*): each and every one without exception

SYNOPSIS

In Lesson 1, we learned that there are different words used in the New Testament to describe *healing*. The first Greek term we saw is *iaomai*, which describes *a progressive kind of healing*. As you pray for someone, the Spirit of God touches them, and from that moment forward they begin to get better. Although this healing is not instantaneous, it is most definitely a supernatural restoration by the hand of God.

The second Greek word for healing that we examined is *therapeuo*, and it is the word used most often to describe the healing ministry of Jesus. It is where we get the word *therapy* and pictures *a healing touch that requires corresponding actions*. Again, this is the primary word used to describe the way Jesus healed the sick. In this lesson, we will continue to explore the methods Jesus used to heal the sick, but let's first review some important things from our first lesson.

The emphasis of this lesson:

Jesus took time to heal people of all kinds of problems, including mental and emotional torments, demonization, palsy, and debilitating conditions that resulted from dabbling in the occult. Multitudes of sick people were brought to Him, and no sickness or disease could stand against Jesus' mighty power.

Jesus Took Time To Heal People of All Kinds of Problems

Our anchor verse for this study is Hebrews 13:8, which declares, "Jesus Christ the same yesterday, and to day, and for ever." This clearly tells us that what Jesus did during His First-Century ministry on earth, is what

He's still doing today and will continue to do until He returns. He is the same Jesus today as He was back then. His character, His compassion, and His actions are the same. Therefore, if Jesus healed people then, He's still healing people now, and the methods He used before are the same ones He is using today.

In Matthew 4:23, the Bible says, "And Jesus went about all Galilee, teaching in their synagogues, and preaching the gospel of the kingdom, and healing all manner of sickness and all manner of disease among the people." The word "healing" in this verse is the Greek word *therapeuo*, which is where we get the word *therapy*. Thus, this verse could literally be translated, "And Jesus went about Galilee… *therapying* all manner of sickness and all manner of disease among the people." Again, this word *therapeuo* depicts *a healing touch that requires corresponding actions.*

The use of this word shows us emphatically that Jesus wasn't in a hurry when He prayed for the sick. His meetings lasted as long as they needed to last, and He carefully and kindly dealt with every person as if he or she was the only one there. Instead of just quickly praying for someone and moving on, Jesus *therapied* them. That is, He required specific corresponding actions of them, which demonstrated their faith and confirmed their healing.

For example, when Jesus prayed for a person with a withered hand, He told them to *stretch it forth*. When He prayed for people who were lame, He told them to *rise up and walk*. As they exercised their will in faith and did what Jesus said, He released His healing power into their life. There are examples like this all throughout the four gospels.

Similarly, if you'll take time to pray for people and tell them to do something — in faith — that they couldn't do previously, you will see more manifestations of God's healing than you've been seeing. That's the way Jesus did it, and it's how He taught His disciples — including us — to do it too.

No Sickness or Disease Could Stand Against Jesus' Mighty Power!

Another important truth we saw in Matthew 4:23 is that Jesus was "healing all manner of sickness and disease." The word "sickness" is the Greek word *nosos*, which describes *a terminal condition for which there is no natural cure.* It's a sickness that is often the result of evil spirits, or we could say these were spirit-inflicted diseases. This category of sickness was deemed the worst and most severe of all sickness. And even though there seemed to be no earthly cure for them, they were not incurable for Jesus.

In addition to healing sicknesses, Scripture says Jesus healed all manner of *disease.* The Greek word for "disease" in this verse is different than the word for sickness. Here, it is the word *malakia,* which describes *a crippling or debilitating form of sickness.* It's something that affects your nerves or muscles and greatly hinders the way you live and function. Matthew noted that Jesus healed these kinds of crippling, debilitating diseases, and as a result, "…His fame went throughout all Syria…" (Matthew 4:24).

We saw in Lesson 1 that the Greek word for "fame" is *akoe,* which is the term for *the ear.* It denotes *ears filled with information,* and in this case, it describes *ears buzzing with rumors or stories* of Jesus' healing power. The stories these people were hearing moved them greatly, "…and they brought unto him all sick people that were taken with divers diseases and torments, and those which were possessed with devils, and those which were lunatick, and those that had the palsy; and he healed them" (Matthew 4:24).

5 Specific Conditions Jesus Healed

Jesus healed *diseases.* The word "diseases" here is the Greek word *nosos,* which describes *a terminal condition for which there is no natural cure,* and in the ancient world, it denoted a sickness that was the result of evil spirits.

Jesus healed *torments.* The original Greek text here actually says "oppressing torments," which is a translation of the words *basanois sunechomenous,* and it depicts *one who is oppressed or tormented.* This phrase signifies *one who is tormented in his mind or his emotions,* which means Jesus has healing power for those who are mentally or emotionally tormented.

Jesus healed those *possessed with devils.* This phrase is a translation of the Greek word *daimonidzomai,* describing *those who were demonized in some area of their life.* To be demon possessed implies that a person is completely possessed and totally controlled by demons, but that's not what this is talking about. The word *daimonidzomai* refers to people who were demonized in a specific area of their life. Jesus recognized this and set them free.

Jesus healed *lunatics*. In Greek, the word for "lunatick" is *seleniadzomai*, and it literally means *moonstruck*. This debilitating condition took place during a full moon, which signified *a sickness resulting from dabbling in the occult*. In Israel there were people who played around with the occult, and according to this verse, those who did so often became sick as a result. Jesus had the power to set them free, and He did.

Jesus healed those with *palsy*. The Greek word for "palsy" is *paralutikos*, which describes *those who were paralyzed*.

What did Jesus do for people dealing with these debilitating issues? The Bible says He "healed" them. Once more we see the Greek word *therapeuo*, translated here as "healed." It is the word for *therapy*, and it pictures *a healing touch that requires corresponding actions*. The use of this word tells us that Jesus took time with these people. For instance, if they were paralyzed, Jesus spoke a word, released the anointing, and said, "Get up; pick up your bed, and walk." He required them to do something to exercise their faith, and as they cooperated with Jesus, the power of God manifested, and bam! They were healed!

Matthew finished the chapter, saying, "And there followed him great multitudes of people from Galilee, and from Decapolis, and from Jerusalem, and from Judaea, and from beyond Jordan" (Matthew 4:25). The rumors and stories of Jesus' healing power buzzing in people's ears drew them from all around the region, and they followed Jesus in droves.

Multitudes of Sick People Were Brought to Jesus and He Healed Them All

Like Matthew, Mark's gospel also documents the droves of people who sought out Jesus to be healed. Mark 1:32 says, "And at even, when the sun did set, they brought unto him all that were diseased, and them that were possessed with devils." The word "brought" here is the Greek word *phero*, which means *to physically carry* like you would carry a piece of furniture, a box, or something heavy. Apparently, these people were so sick that they were invalids, unable to walk to where Jesus was. Out of great love, their family and friends physically picked them up and carried them to Jesus.

The people who were carried included "...all that were diseased, and them that were possessed with devils" (Mark 1:32). Notice the word "all." It is the Greek word *pantas*, meaning *absolutely all*, which tells us that absolutely every debilitating disease responded obediently to the authority of Jesus!

In this verse, the word "diseased" is *echo kakos*, which means *miserably afflicted* or *extremely sick*. It is a phrase that was used to describe *a person in the last stage of their condition* or *a terminal case*. These individuals were among the many people who were brought to Jesus to be healed. Still others were "possessed with devils," which again is the Greek word *daimonidzomai*, describing *those who were demonized*.

The Bible goes on to say, "And all the city was gathered together at the door. And he [Jesus] healed many that were sick of divers diseases, and cast out many devils…" (Mark 1:33,34). Can you guess what Greek word is used for "healed"? If you said *therapeuo*, you are correct. Again, we see that Jesus *therapied* those who came to Him, requiring corresponding actions from them to see His healing manifested in their bodies.

And how many people were healed? Mark 1:34 says "many" — the Greek word *polus*, meaning *many* or *vast multitudes*. Thus, Jesus therapied vast multitudes of individuals, taking time to work with each one in order for His healing power to fully manifest in their bodies. These were individuals that the Bible categorized as "sick of divers diseases."

The word "sick" here is the Greek word *kakos*, which means *sick in a bad, foul way*. This type of sickness is often associated with demonic activity. The words "divers diseases" form the phrase *poikilos nosos*, respectively. The word "divers" (*poikilos*) describes *something assorted, divers, multiple,* or *various*. It's the same word used in the Septuagint to describe Joseph's coat of many colors. The Greek word for "diseases" here is *nosos*, which denotes *a terminal condition for which there is no natural cure*. The use of these words tells us that the types of terminal diseases these people were dealing with were of multiple shades and colors. Yet, all of them submitted to the authority of Jesus.

Jesus Also 'Cast Out Many Devils'

In addition to healing people of multiple kinds of foul sicknesses, the Bible says Jesus also "…cast out many devils…" (Mark 1:34). In Greek, the phrase "cast out" is the word *ekballo*, a compound of the words *ek* and *ballo*. The word *ek* means *out* and is where we get the word *exit* from, and the word *ballo* means *to throw*, as in throwing a ball or rock. When these words are compounded to form the new word *ekballo*, it means *to throw out, cast out,* or *forcibly evict.* The use of these words, along with the word *therapuo* (healed), helps us see that Jesus was not in a hurry when He ran into demonically induced diseases. He stood toe-to-toe with them and forcefully evicted those demons from people's lives.

Although many believers don't talk about devils, they are real, and Jesus encountered them in His earthly ministry. In fact, Scripture says He cast out "many devils." The word "many" is the Greek word *polus*, which we saw earlier in the same verse. It means *many* or *vast multitudes.* And the word "devils" is a translation of the Greek word *daimonion,* which describes *evil spirits, demons,* or *devils.* The ancient world generally believed demons thickly populated the lower regions of the air and that spirits were the primary cause of disasters and suffering in the earth. Moreover, this word *daimonion* could depict a person deemed *insane,* and in both secular and New Testament writings, it depicted those possessed with evil spirits who suffered from spirit-inflicted mental or physical infirmities.

The gospels tell us repeatedly that Jesus cast out devils. This is recorded not only in Mark 1:34 but also in Mark 1:39, where Mark wrote, "And he [Jesus] preached in their synagogues throughout all Galilee, and cast out devils." The word "devils" here is *daimonion,* the same word used in verse 34, which describes *evil spirits, demons,* or *devils.* Scripture says that Jesus "cast out" — *ekballo* — these evil spirits. That is, He *forcefully evicted* them from people's lives.

Luke Also Cites Jesus' Therapeutic Healing

Indeed, Jesus' healing ministry is highlighted in all the gospels, including Luke 4:40, where Luke wrote, "Now when the sun was setting, all they that had any sick with divers diseases brought them unto him; and he laid his hands on every one of them, and healed them." In this verse, the word "sick" is the Greek word *astheneia,* which is an all-encompassing term for *all types of sickness and disease.* The word "divers" in Greek is again the word *poikilos,* which describes *assorted, divers,* or *various diseases,* and the Greek word for "diseases" is *nosos,* the word describing *a terminal condition for which there is no natural cure.* It was a sickness that was the result of evil spirits.

Luke specifically documented that Jesus laid His hands on "…every one of them, and healed them" (Luke 4:40). The words "every one" are a translation of the Greek word *hekastos,* which describes *each and every one without exception*. And the word Luke used for "healed" is again *therapeuo* — the Greek word for *therapy*. This tells us that regardless of how big the crowd was, Jesus took time to lay His hands on every single person and work with them until healing manifested.

Friend, God wants to manifest His healing power in people's lives through *your* hands. If you have been disappointed by the results you've seen when praying for people to be healed, begin to implement the same practices Jesus used in His healing ministry. Pray and declare God's healing over their lives then work with them to see His restoration fully manifested. Ask them to do something they couldn't do before to demonstrate their faith and cooperate with God's therapeutic power, and greater results will follow!

STUDY QUESTIONS

Study to shew thyself approved unto God, a workman that needeth not to be ashamed, rightly dividing the word of truth.
— 2 Timothy 2:15

1. Jesus' way of healing people and His instructions to them varied widely and didn't always make sense — but they worked! What is one of the strangest healings Jesus did that you can think of? Consider the healing documented in John 9:1-11. What did Jesus do and what did He ask a blind man to do in order to receive his healing?

2. What do you notice about the disciples' question regarding the man who had been born blind? How about Jesus' response to their question? What else does He go on to say? How does this change your view of how we should approach healing in these last days?

3. The Bible points out that there are certain sicknesses that result from dabbling in the occult. Occult practices include participating in seances, using tarot cards and Ouija boards, seeking direction from fortune tellers and mediums, and spirit cooking. If you've been involved in any occult practice like these, you have opened a door to the realm of darkness. But if you'll pray and ask God to forgive you, Jesus will set you free from any demonically induced sickness or disease. Take time now to make things right with the Lord (*see* 1 John 1:9).

PRACTICAL APPLICATION

But be ye doers of the word, and not hearers only,
deceiving your own selves.
—James 1:22

1. How does it feel to know that Jesus has healed every kind of sickness
    and disease? How does it give you hope for your own restoration or
    hope to see someone you love healed?

2. Where in your life do you need healing? Get quiet and ask the Holy
    Spirit to begin to show you what your part is in order to receive your
    healing. Also, ask Him to give you the grace you need to start taking
    those steps.

3. As you practice praying for your healing and the healing of others,
    remember to keep your ears and eyes open and watch for the Holy
    Spirit to lead you. Begin to take the steps He shows you; journal what
    comes to your heart and watch His healing manifest in your life and
    in the lives of those around you.

TOPIC

Examples of 'Therapy' in the Healing Ministry of Jesus

SCRIPTURES

1. **Hebrews 13:8** — Jesus Christ the same yesterday, and to day, and for
    ever.

2. **John 21:25** — And there are also many other things which Jesus did,
    the which, if they should be written every one, I suppose that even
    the world itself could not contain the books that should be written.
    Amen.

3. **Matthew 12:9-14** — And when he was departed thence, he went into
    their synagogue: And, behold, there was a man which had his hand
    withered. And they asked him, saying, Is it lawful to heal on the sab-
    bath days? that they might accuse him. And he said unto them, What

man shall there be among you, that shall have one sheep, and if it fall into a pit on the sabbath day, will he not lay hold on it, and lift it out? How much then is a man better than a sheep? Wherefore it is lawful to do well on the sabbath days. Then saith he to the man, Stretch forth thine hand. And he stretched it forth; and it was restored whole, like as the other. Then the Pharisees went out, and held a council against him, how they might destroy him.

4. **John 5:1-11** — After this there was a feast of the Jews; and Jesus went up to Jerusalem. Now there is at Jerusalem by the sheep market a pool, which is called in the Hebrew tongue Bethesda, having five porches. In these lay a great multitude of impotent folk, of blind, halt, withered, waiting for the moving of the water. For an angel went down at a certain season into the pool, and troubled the water: whosoever then first after the troubling of the water stepped in was made whole of whatsoever disease he had. And a certain man was there, which had an infirmity thirty and eight years. When Jesus saw him lie, and knew that he had been now a long time in that case, he saith unto him, Wilt thou be made whole? The impotent man answered him, Sir, I have no man, when the water is troubled, to put me into the pool: but while I am coming, another steppeth down before me. Jesus saith unto him, Rise, take up thy bed, and walk. And immediately the man was made whole, and took up his bed, and walked: and on the same day was the sabbath. The Jews therefore said unto him that was cured, It is the sabbath day: it is not lawful for thee to carry thy bed. He answered them, He that made me whole, the same said unto me, Take up thy bed, and walk.

5. **Acts 3:1-8** — Now Peter and John went up together into the temple at the hour of prayer, being the ninth hour. And a certain man lame from his mother's womb was carried, whom they laid daily at the gate of the temple which is called Beautiful, to ask alms of them that entered into the temple; Who seeing Peter and John about to go into the temple asked an alms. And Peter, fastening his eyes upon him with John, said, Look on us. And he gave heed unto them, expecting to receive something of them. Then Peter said, Silver and gold have I none; but such as I have give I thee: In the name of Jesus Christ of Nazareth rise up and walk. And he took him by the right hand, and lifted him up: and immediately his feet and ankle bones received strength. And he leaping up stood, and walked, and entered with them into the temple, walking, and leaping, and praising God.

GREEK WORDS

1. "heal" — **θεραπεύω** (*therapeuo*): therapy; pictures a healing touch that requires corresponding actions

2. "stretch forth" — **ἐκτείνω** (*ekteino*): compound of **ἐκ** (*ek*) and **τείνω** (*teino*); the preposition **ἐκ** (*ek*) means out, and the word **τείνω** (*teino*) means to stretch; compounded, to strenuously stretch out; to put forth one's full effort to stretch out [his arm or hand]

3. "stretched it forth" — **ἐξέτεινεν** (*exeteinen*): to strenuously stretch out; put forth his full effort to stretch out [his arm or hand]

4. "restored" — **ἀποκαθίστημι** (*apokathistemi*): restored back to its original condition

5. "whole" **ὑγιής** (*hugies*): healthy; sound; whole

6. "impotent folk" — **ἀσθένεια** (*astheneia*): an all-encompassing term for all types of sickness and disease

7. "blind" — **τυφλός** (*tuphlos*): blind; not only blind, but even includes those who have no eyes with which to see

8. "halt" — **χωλός** (*cholos*): maimed, likely due to an accident

9. "withered" — **ξηρός** (*xeros*): unprofitable; useless eaters; pictures those who contribute nothing to society; where we derive the word zero

10. "Sir" — **Κύριε** (*Kurie*): direct form of **κύριος** (*kurios*); Supreme Master

11. "rise" — **Ἔγειρε** (*egeire*): to rise; to get up; root word for resurrection

12. "take up" — **αἴρω** (*airo*): to pick up; related to a word for muscular ability; use all you've got to pick up that bed

13. "bed" — **κράβαττος** (*krabattos*): mattress on which he was lying

14. "walk" — **περιπατέω** (*peripateo*): to walk around; to get moving

15. "was" — **ἐγένετο** (*egeneto*): pictures progress

16. "cured" — **θεραπεύω** (*therapeuo*): therapy; pictures a healing touch that requires corresponding actions

17. "lame" — **χωλὸς** (*cholos*): damaged; disfigured; injured; maimed

18. "rise up" — **αἴρω** (*airo*): to pick up; related to a word for muscular ability; meaning 'use all you've got to rise and pick up that bed'

19. "took" — **πιάζω** (*piadzo*): to arrest; to apprehend; to forcibly lay hold of; to seize

20. "lifted him up" — **αἴρω** (*airo*): to pick up; related to a word for muscular ability; to put forth all his strength to physically pull him up

21. "feet" — **αἱ βάσεις** (*hai baseis*): steps; pictures him taking one step at a time

22. "received strength" — **ἐστερεώθησαν** (*estereothesan*): were progressively strengthened [as they walked him]

SYNOPSIS

Did you know that there are examples of "therapy" in Jesus' healing ministry all throughout the gospels? It's true. The man with the withered hand in Matthew 12 and the paralytic at the pool of Bethesda in John 5 are two great examples where Jesus took time to work with the sick to receive their full healing. Rather than pray a quick prayer and walk away, Jesus gave individuals specific instructions, requiring them to do something in faith to cooperate with His healing power. We see the same thing take place when Peter and John brought healing to the lame man in Acts 3.

In this lesson, we will study these three examples of Jesus' therapeutic healing more closely to see what new insights we can learn and how we can apply this wisdom in our own ministry to others.

The emphasis of this lesson:

The man with the withered hand, the paralytic at the pool of Bethesda, and the lame man at the Temple each received their healing progressively as they cooperated with the *therapeuo* power of God working in their life.

A Quick Review

Jesus is the same. Hebrews 13:8 powerfully states, "Jesus Christ the same yesterday, and to day, and for ever." Whatever Jesus did then, He's still doing now. He healed people of all kinds of sicknesses and diseases then, and He's still healing people of all types of sicknesses and diseases today. We don't have to wonder if it is still His will to heal people. It is because Jesus is the same!

The magnitude of Jesus' miracles is voluminous. John 21:25 tells us, "…There are also many other things which Jesus did, the which, if they should be written every one, I suppose that even the world itself could not contain the books that should be written. Amen." When we read this in the original Greek text, it says, "There were so many miracles that Jesus did that we cannot write them all down, but I suppose *if* it were possible to write them, the world itself could not contain the books that could be written."

If you had been with Jesus, walking with His disciples, you would never have been bored. There was always something to see! At every turn and in every town, He manifested some kind of healing and miracle in people's lives. From turning water into wine to casting out demons to walking on water to raising the dead, the supernatural power of God was on display through Jesus' life all the time.

Jesus sometimes healed people gradually. We've seen that one of the words for *healing* in the New Testament is the Greek word *iaomai*, which means *to cure* or *to heal*. This word describes *a progressive kind of healing that happens over a period of time*. An example of the use of *iaomai* is found in Acts 10:38, where it says, "…God anointed Jesus of Nazareth with the Holy Ghost and with power: who went about doing good, and *healing* all that were oppressed of the devil; for God was with him."

Most often, when Jesus healed someone, He required corresponding actions. This kind of healing is depicted in the word *therapeuo* — the word used most often in the gospels to describe Jesus' healing ministry. It's where we get the word *therapy* from, and it depicts *a healing touch that requires corresponding actions*. Rather than just praying for someone and saying, "You're healed," and then walking away, the word *therapeuo* pictures Jesus staying long enough to work with the person until his or her healing manifested. He didn't leave people alone to figure it out themselves.

The Man With the 'Withered' Hand

Our first example of the word *therapeuo* is found in Matthew 12:9-14. The Bible says, "And when he was departed thence, he went into their synagogue: And, behold, there was a man which had his hand withered…" (Matthew 12:9,10). Here we see Jesus enter a synagogue, one of the holiest of places in the Jewish world, and He saw a man whose hand was *withered*. This word "withered" is a translation of the Greek word *xeros*, which is where we get the word *zero*. Whatever had happened to this man's hand had caused it to become totally useless — a *zero*-factor in his life.

Scripture goes on to say, "…And they asked him, saying, Is it lawful to heal on the sabbath days? that they might accuse him" (Matthew 12:10). Obviously, it's lawful and right to pray for anyone on the Sabbath day, but the religious leaders were specifically asking Jesus if it was lawful to heal on the Sabbath. The word "heal" used here is the word *therapeuo*, which means they were asking, "Is it lawful to *therapy* the sick on the Sabbath day?" They knew that when Jesus released this kind of healing power, people had to put forth effort and work with Him to be healed.

According to the Jewish leaders, absolutely no work of any kind could be done on the Sabbath. They were familiar with Jesus' healing services and knew He would stay with people and work with them one on one until their healing manifested. Thus, these leaders asked Jesus if it was lawful not only for Him to perform the healing, but also for the people to exert energy to experience their healing.

How did Jesus handle the situation? The Bible says, "And he [Jesus] said unto them, What man shall there be among you, that shall have one sheep, and if it fall into a pit on the sabbath day, will he not lay hold on it, and lift it out? How much then is a man better than a sheep? Wherefore it is lawful to do well on the sabbath days. Then saith he to the man, Stretch forth thine hand. And he stretched it forth; and it was restored whole, like as the other" (Matthew 12:11-13).

Here we see that Jesus required the man with the withered hand to do something. He said, "Stretch forth your hand." In Greek, the phrase "stretch forth" is the word *ekteino*, a compound of *ek* and *teino*. The preposition *ek* means *out*, and the word *teino* means *to stretch*. When compounded, the new word *ekteino* means *to strenuously stretch out* and *to put forth one's full effort to stretch out* [in this case his arm or hand]. Without question, what Jesus asked this man to do was very difficult and painful. Basically, He told the man, "Put forth all the effort you have and cooperate with Me. Do what you normally couldn't do — stretch out your hand," and the Bible says he stretched it out.

This is a remarkable picture of how Jesus *therapied* people. He didn't just say, "You're healed." He required the man to cooperate in faith to receive his healing, and when he did, the man's hand was "restored." In Greek, the word "restored" is *apokathistemi*, which means *restored back to its original condition*. It carries the idea of something that happens *progressively*, which means the man was not instantly healed but gradually healed. Had he not cooperated with Jesus, he wouldn't have received healing.

Matthew 12:14 says, "Then the Pharisees went out, and held a council against him, how they might destroy him." In their eyes, Jesus was requiring people like this man with the withered hand to put forth effort and "work" on the Sabbath, which was against the law and one more reason they wanted to do away with Him.

The Paralytic at the Pool

Moving to John's gospel, we find another example of Jesus' therapeutic healing. The Bible says, "After this there was a feast of the Jews; and Jesus went up to Jerusalem. Now there is at Jerusalem by the sheep market a pool, which is called in the Hebrew tongue Bethesda, having five porches. In these lay a great multitude of impotent folk, of blind, halt, withered, waiting for the moving of the water" (John 5:1-3).

Notice the name of this legendary pool is "Bethesda," which could be translated "The House of Mercy," "The House of Goodness," or "The House of Grace." Bethesda was known among the Jews as a place where God's mercy, His goodness, and His grace showed up and blessed people. This is why "…a great multitude of impotent folk, of blind, halt, withered, [were gathered] waiting for the moving of the water" (John 5:3). In Greek, the words "impotent folk" are the word *astheneia*, an all-encompassing term for *all types of sickness and disease* — especially invalids and those bedridden.

The next group at Bethesda was the "blind." This word is a translation of the Greek word *tuphlos*, which describes not only *blind*, but even *those who have no eyes with which to see*. The Greek word for "halt" is *cholos*, and it denotes those *maimed*, likely due to an accident. John then said the "withered" were there. This word "withered" is the same Greek word we saw in Matthew 12:10 — the word *xeros*, which is where we derive the word *zero*. It describes *unprofitable, useless eaters*. Moreover, it pictures those who are unable to contribute anything to society because of their broken condition.

Why were all these sick and broken people at Bethesda? They were waiting for something. Scripture says, "For an angel went down at a certain season into the pool, and troubled the water: whosoever then first after the troubling of the water stepped in was made whole of whatsoever disease he had. And a certain man was there, which had an infirmity thirty and eight years. When Jesus saw him lie, and knew that he had been now a long time in that case, he saith unto him, Wilt thou be made whole? The impotent man answered him, Sir, I have no man, when the water is troubled, to put me into the pool: but while I am coming, another steppeth down before me" (John 5:4-7).

Here we see a bedfast man who for nearly four decades was trying to receive his healing, but because he couldn't get into the pool first, he remained disabled and confined to the sideline. In that divine moment, Jesus — the Great Creator and Healer — was standing before him. The lame man saw something magnificent in Jesus and addressed Him as "Sir," which is the Greek word *Kurie* and is capitalized. It is a direct form of *kurios*, the word meaning *Supreme Master*. Using this title was the equivalent of telling Jesus, "Lord, I will do whatever You say because You are the Supreme Master." When Jesus heard this address, He knew He had authority to speak into this man's life.

In that moment, "Jesus saith unto him, Rise, take up thy bed, and walk" (John 5:8). "Rise" is the Greek word *egeire*, which means *to rise* or *to get up*; it's the root word for *resurrection*. Just as it's impossible to raise the dead unless you're a believer, it was physically and naturally impossible for this man to *rise up*. Yet Jesus said, "Get up and take up your bed." The words "take up" are a translation of the word *airo*, which means *to pick up*. Interestingly, it's a term related to a Greek word that describes using all of one's *muscular ability* to do something. Hence, its use here is the equivalent of Jesus saying, "Use all your muscular ability to pick up your bed and walk."

The word "bed" in this verse is the Greek word *krabattos*, which describes *the mattress on which he was lying*. And the word "walk" is the Greek word *peripateo*, which means *to walk around in a circle*. Here, it is essentially a command to *get moving*. But how in the world was this paralyzed man going to get moving? How was he going to physically pick up his mattress? He couldn't even stand on his own two feet. Nevertheless, when Jesus showed up at Bethesda, healing opportunity was knocking exclusively at this lame man's door. In obedience and great faith, the man summoned all the muscular strength his feeble body possessed and made the effort to get up.

The Bible says, "And immediately the man was made whole, and took up his bed, and walked…" (John 5:9). Notice the word "was." It is the Greek word *egeneto*, which pictures *progress* and describes *something that happens progressively*. As this man put forth all the effort he had to cooperate with Jesus, he began to progressively become whole, and he took up his bed and walked! Curiously, the Bible adds, "…And on the same day was the sabbath. The Jews therefore said unto him that was cured, It is the sabbath day: it is not lawful for thee to carry thy bed. He answered them, He that made me whole, the same said unto me, Take up thy bed, and walk" (John 5:9-11). John wrote that the man was "cured." Once more, this is the familiar Greek word *therapeuo*, describing *therapy* and picturing a *healing touch that requires corresponding actions.* Jesus *therapied* this lame man and fully restored his legs.

The Lame Man at the Temple

A third example of this Greek word *therapeuo* involves the apostles Peter and John. The Bible says, "Now Peter and John went up together into the temple at the hour of prayer, being the ninth hour. And a certain man lame from his mother's womb was carried, whom they laid daily at the gate of the temple which is called Beautiful, to ask alms of them that entered into the temple" (Acts 3:1,2).

The word "lame" in verse 2 is the Greek word *cholos*, and it describes *one damaged, disfigured, injured,* or *maimed.* This man had been born in this condition, and every day his family members or friends would physically carry him to the Temple and place him in front of the Gate Beautiful to beg for money.

Scripture goes on to say, "Who seeing Peter and John about to go into the temple asked an alms. And Peter, fastening his eyes upon him with John, said, Look on us. And he gave heed unto them, expecting to receive something of them. Then Peter said, Silver and gold have I none; but such as I have give I thee: In the name of Jesus Christ of Nazareth rise up and walk" (Acts 3:3-6).

Please note that Peter and John didn't just say, "You're healed," and keep walking. On the contrary, they were disciples of Jesus, and they did what they had seen Him do countless times. They knew this man needed to cooperate and release his faith, which is why they said, "Rise up!" This is a translation of the Greek word *airo* — the same word Jesus used at Bethesda. It means *to pick up* and is related to the Greek term that describes *using all of one's muscular ability to do something.* The word "walk" is the Greek word *peripateo*, which means *to walk around* or *to get moving.* Basically, Peter and Paul looked at the lame man and said, "Use all your muscular ability to pick yourself up and get moving."

Acts 3:7 and 8 then tells us, "And he took him by the right hand, and lifted him up: and immediately his feet and ankle bones received strength. And he leaping up stood, and walked, and entered with them into the temple, walking, and leaping, and praising God." The word "took" is the Greek word *piadzo*, which means *to arrest, to apprehend, to forcibly lay hold of*, or *to seize*. The use of this word *piadzo* (took) tells us this lame man didn't immediately receive his healing.

To assist him, Peter and John intentionally laid hold of his hand and "lifted him up." Here again is the Greek word *airo*, meaning *to pick up*. In this case, we find Peter on one side and John on the other, each *using all their muscular ability to lift this man up from the ground and to his feet*. When we read this verse in the Greek, it says, "Immediately his *steps* received strength," which means *they were literally walking with this man*.

The word "feet" in Greek is *hai baseis*, which describes *steps*. It pictures this man taking one step at a time. Peter and John were walking with this man, and with each new step, the man's feet (steps) and ankle bones progressively "received strength." This phrase literally means *they were progressively strengthened* [as Peter and John walked him]. If Peter and John hadn't walked him, and if the lame man hadn't been willing to cooperate, he likely would have remained at the Gate Beautiful begging for money the rest of his life. But because Peter and John *therapied* him just like they had seen Jesus do, the man was restored, and God received great glory.

STUDY QUESTIONS

> **Study to shew thyself approved unto God, a workman that needeth not to be ashamed, rightly dividing the word of truth.**
> **— 2 Timothy 2:15**

1. The healing of the lame man at the Gate Beautiful was so much more involved than most of us have probably imagined, especially the fact that Peter and John actually walked with him until his healing manifested. His healing required his own cooperation, God's power, and the help of others. Who else had people that played a vital part in them receiving their healing? (Read Mark 2:1-12; Luke 5:17-26.) What stands out to you about this story?

2. According to Acts 9:32-42, who else was restored by Peter's instructions to "rise up"? In your own words, explain what happened. What were the far-reaching results of her restoration (*see* verse 42)?

PRACTICAL APPLICATION

1. Of the three biblical accounts — the man with the withered hand, the paralytic at the pool of Bethesda, and the lame man at the Temple — which one did you gain the most new insights from? What details were most surprising for you to learn? How does this expand your understanding of Jesus' power to heal?

2. Who in your life do you know needs healing or even resurrection in an area of their life? Commit to pray for their situation, "carrying" them to Jesus. Listen for the Holy Spirit's instructions and watch His power begin to work in their life. It may happen gradually, but your efforts will make a difference!

3. Going back to the beginning of the lesson, we learned that Jesus never ever left someone alone to figure out their own healing process. Instead, He stayed and worked with them until they were truly whole. How does knowing this give you peace and encouragement?

LESSON 4

TOPIC

Other Insights Into Healing

SCRIPTURES

1. **Hebrews 13:8** — Jesus Christ the same yesterday, and to day, and for ever.

2. **John 21:25** — And there are also many other things which Jesus did, the which, if they should be written every one, I suppose that even the world itself could not contain the books that should be written. Amen.

3. **Mark 5:21-42** — And when Jesus was passed over again by ship
    unto the other side, much people gathered unto him: and he was
    nigh unto the sea. And, behold, there cometh one of the rulers of the
    synagogue, Jairus by name; and when he saw him, he fell at his feet,
    and besought him greatly, saying, My little daughter lieth at the point
    of death: I pray thee, come and lay thy hands on her, that she may be
    healed; and she shall live. And Jesus went with him; and much people
    followed him, and thronged him. And a certain woman, which had
    an issue of blood twelve years, and had suffered many things of many
    physicians, and had spent all that she had, and was nothing bettered,
    but rather grew worse, when she had heard of Jesus, came in the
    press behind, and touched his garment. For she said, If I may touch
    but his clothes, I shall be whole. And straightway the fountain of her
    blood was dried up; and she felt in her body that she was healed of
    that plague. And Jesus, immediately knowing in himself that virtue
    had gone out of him, turned him about in the press, and said, Who
    touched my clothes? And his disciples said unto him, Thou seest the
    multitude thronging thee, and sayest thou, Who touched me? And
    he looked round about to see her that had done this thing. But the
    woman fearing and trembling, knowing what was done in her, came
    and fell down before him, and told him all the truth. And he said
    unto her, Daughter, thy faith hath made thee whole; go in peace, and
    be whole of thy plague. While he yet spake, there came from the ruler
    of the synagogue's house certain which said, Thy daughter is dead:
    why troublest thou the Master any further? As soon as Jesus heard
    the word that was spoken, he saith unto the ruler of the synagogue,
    Be not afraid, only believe. And he suffered no man to follow him,
    save Peter, and James, and John the brother of James. And he cometh
    to the house of the ruler of the synagogue, and seeth the tumult, and
    them that wept and wailed greatly. And when he was come in, he
    saith unto them, Why make ye this ado, and weep? the damsel is not
    dead, but sleepeth. And they laughed him to scorn. But when he had
    put them all out, he taketh the father and the mother of the damsel,
    and them that were with him, and entereth in where the damsel was
    lying. And he took the damsel by the hand, and said unto her, Talitha
    cumi; which is, being interpreted, Damsel, I say unto thee, arise. And
    straightway the damsel arose, and walked; for she was of the age of
    twelve years. And they were astonished with a great astonishment.

4. **Leviticus 15:19-27** — And if a woman have an issue, and her issue in her flesh be blood, she shall be put apart seven days: and whosoever toucheth her shall be unclean until the even. And every thing that she lieth upon in her separation shall be unclean: every thing also that she sitteth upon shall be unclean. And whosoever toucheth her bed shall wash his clothes, and bathe himself in water, and be unclean until the even. And whosoever toucheth any thing that she sat upon shall wash his clothes, and bathe himself in water, and be unclean until the even. And if it be on her bed, or on any thing whereon she sitteth, when he toucheth it, he shall be unclean until the even. And if any man lie with her at all, and her flowers be upon him, he shall be unclean seven days; and all the bed whereon he lieth shall be unclean. And if a woman have an issue of her blood many days out of the time of her separation, or if it run beyond the time of her separation; all the days of the issue of her uncleanness shall be as the days of her separation: she shall be unclean. Every bed whereon she lieth all the days of her issue shall be unto her as the bed of her separation: and whatsoever she sitteth upon shall be unclean, as the uncleanness of her separation. And whosoever toucheth those things shall be unclean, and shall wash his clothes, and bathe himself in water, and be unclean until the even.

GREEK WORDS

1. "much people" — ὄχλος πολύς (*ochlus polus*): a large crowd; a vast multitude; a massive crowd

2. "fell" — πίπτω (*pipto*): to fall; to collapse

3. "besought" — παρακαλέω (*parakaleo*): to beg intensely; to plead

4. "saying" — λέγων (*legon*): saying, saying, and saying

5. "lieth at the point of death" — ἐσχάτως (*eschatos*): is at the very end of her journey; end of her sickness

6. "healed" — σῴζω (*sodzo*): salvation; wholeness in every part of life; a touch of salvation that brings delivering and healing power that results in wholeness

7. "thronged" — θλῖψις (*thlipsis*): to suffocate; to crush

8. "issue" — ῥύσις (*rhusis*): a flowing stream

9. "suffered" — πάθος (*pathos*): includes mental or emotional suffering

10. "of" — ὑπὸ (*hupo*): under; under the care or oversight of

11. "spent" — **δαπανάω** (*dapanao*): to squander; to spend with great effort

12. "the things" — **τὰ περὶ** (*ta peri*): things about; things concerning; things revolving around

13. "said" — **ἔλεγεν** (*elegen*): said, said, and kept on saying

14. "whole" — **σῴζω** (*sodzo*): salvation; wholeness in every part of life; a touch of salvation that brings delivering and healing power that results in wholeness

15. "fountain" — **πηγή** (*pege*): fountain; spring; rushing fountain

16. "healed" — **ἰάομαι** (*iaomai*): cured; doctored; progressively healed

17. "plague" — **μάστιγος** (*mastigos*): plague; a word borrowed from the world of torture; denoted the act of recurrently beating a prisoner or victim; once a person's wounds had mended, the torturers brought him back to the whipping post, where he was struck again and again and again; such beatings were sporadic but constant, and although they were not usually serious enough to kill, it kept a victim in constant pain and misery; torment and abuse that caused great suffering and prolonged anguish; depicts a recurring sickness or physical affliction that keeps a sufferer in a protracted, repeated state of suffering

18. "knowing" — **ἐπιγινώσκω** (*epiginosko*): expertise; knowledge

19. "virtue" — **δύναμις** (*dunamis*): power; explosive, superhuman power that comes with enormous energy and produces phenomenal, extraordinary, and unparalleled results; the word depicts "mighty deeds" that are impressive, incomparable, and beyond human ability to perform; denotes miraculous power or miraculous manifestations

20. "looked round about" — **περιβλέπομαι** (*periblepomai*): to look around; to look in a circle

21. "Be not afraid, only believe" — **Μὴ φοβοῦ, μόνον πίστευε** (*me phobou, monon pisteue*): do not give into fear, but I charge you to only believe

22. "tumult" — **θόρυβος** (*thorubos*): commotion and noise; it was common to hire flute players and others who performed public lamentations, so the haunting sound of the flute became synonymous with death and mourning

23. "ado" — **θόρυβος** (*thorubos*): commotion and noise; it was common to hire flute players and others who performed public lamentations, so

the haunting sound of the flute became synonymous with death and mourning

24. "laughed…to scorn" — **καταγελάω** (*katagelao*): laughed; mocked; ridiculed

25. "put them all out" — **ἐκβάλλω** (*ekballo*): to cast out; to throw out; to forcibly evict

SYNOPSIS

As we've noted in our first three lessons, "Jesus Christ [is] the same yester-day, and to day, and for ever" (Hebrews 13:8). What the New Testament documents He did during His earthly ministry are the same things He desires to do through us today. He was in the healing business then, and He's still in the healing business now. The apostle John said, "…There are also many other things which Jesus did, the which, if they should be written every one, I suppose that even the world itself could not contain the books that should be written. Amen" (John 21:25).

Two remarkable healings Jesus did are recorded in three of the four gospels, and they both happened on the same day. The first one is the miraculous healing of the woman with the issue of blood, and the second is the resurrection of Jairus' daughter from the dead. What additional insights about healing can we learn from these examples, and how might they apply to the situations we are facing today? We will discover the answers to these questions in this lesson.

The emphasis of this lesson:

When Jairus' daughter was on the brink of death, Jairus sought Jesus to come and heal her. At the same time, a woman with a longstanding bleeding disorder also sought Jesus for healing. Through faith and per-sistence, they both received the restoration they longed for.

Jairus Sought Jesus
To Bring 'Healing' to His Daughter

Turning to the gospel of Mark, the Bible says, "And when Jesus was passed over again by ship unto the other side, much people gathered unto him: and he was nigh unto the sea" (Mark 5:21). The words "much people" are a translation of the Greek words *ochlus polus*, which describes *a large crowd, a vast multitude,* or *a massive crowd.* Even though Jesus regularly told the people He healed not to tell anyone what He did, word always seemed to get out, and the results were massive crowds that followed Him everywhere He went.

The passage continues, saying, "And, behold, there cometh one of the rulers of the synagogue, Jairus by name; and when he saw him, he fell at his feet" (Mark 5:22). The word "behold" is the Greek word *idou*, and it indicates *awe, amazement,* and *bewilderment.* Mark was utterly shocked at the fact that a high-ranking Jewish official would seek out Jesus for help. Imagine it: a leader of the synagogue all decked out in his beautiful, royal attire came to Jesus and fell at His feet. The word "fell" here is the Greek word *pipto*, meaning *to fall* or *to collapse.* In great desperation, Jairus collapsed like a corpse at Jesus' feet.

Scripture goes on to say, "And besought him greatly, saying, My little daughter lieth at the point of death: I pray thee, come and lay thy hands on her, that she may be healed; and she shall live" (Mark 5:23). There are several key words in this passage, including the word "besought." This is the Greek word *parakaleo*, a compound of the word *para*, meaning *to be alongside of*, and the word *kaleo*, meaning *to call out.* When these words are compounded to form *parakaleo*, it means *to come alongside someone and beg intensely* or *to plead.*

Jairus came right up to Jesus, "…saying, My little daughter lieth at the point of death…" (Mark 5:23). The word "saying" here is the Greek word *legon*, and its tense conveys ongoing activity. Thus, a better translation here would be that Jairus was *saying and saying and saying,* "…My little daughter lieth at the point of death…" (Mark 5:23). The phrase "lieth at the point of death" is a translation of the Greek word *eschatos*, and it means *being at the very end of her journey* or *the end of her sickness.* From these words we see that Jairus collapsed at Jesus' feet and kept on saying and saying, "My little girl is at the very end of her life! She doesn't have much time left. I beg You, come and lay Your hands on her, that she may be healed; and she shall live."

Now, it's unlikely that Jairus had ever attended any of Jesus' meetings because it would not have been proper for him to go. The Jews at that time would have seen Jesus as a rebel, so as a leader of a synagogue, Jairus would have kept a distance from Jesus. However, with his daughter on the brink of death, he became so desperate that he threw off what others thought of him and was willing to do anything to save his little girl's life.

The fact that Jairus told Jesus, "…I pray thee, come and lay thy hands on her, that she may be healed; and she shall live" (Mark 5:23), tells us that he had heard stories of what Jesus had done with His hands. All four gospels bear witness that Jesus had a reputation for touching people and restoring them to health. It was these stories that instilled hope in Jairus that his daughter could be *healed*.

This word "healed" in Mark 5:23 is the Greek word *sodzo*, which is used throughout the New Testament to describe *salvation*. In the Jewish mind, when they heard the word *sodzo*, they equated it with *wholeness in every part of life*. In addition to describing eternal salvation, *sodzo* was seen as a supernatural touch that brings delivering and healing power that results in overall wholeness. As a theologically trained leader of a synagogue, Jairus knew healing belonged to God's people, and that's what he sought for his daughter.

The Woman With the 'Issue of Blood' Was Dealing With Numerous Challenges

The Bible says, "And Jesus went with him; and much people followed him, and thronged him" (Mark 5:24). The word "thronged" here in Greek is *thlipsis*, which means *to suffocate* or *to crush*. Thus, on the way to Jairus' home, Jesus was being suffocated and crushed by a mob of people trying to touch Him. Then something unexpected took place. Amidst the madness of the moment, "…a certain woman, which had an issue of blood twelve years" (Mark 5:25) reached out and touched Jesus. The word "issue" here is extremely important. It is the Greek word *rhusis*, which describes *a flowing stream*. The use of this word indicates this precious woman had a very serious problem, and she had been trying to manage it for twelve years.

Now, you may have read about or heard messages regarding this woman. But what you may not know is the scope of all the exhausting challenges she was dealing with due to her condition. To understand the depth of her dilemma, we turn to the book of Leviticus and the guidelines given by God to Moses concerning women with an issue of blood. Leviticus 15:19 says, "And if a woman have an issue, and her issue in her flesh be blood, she shall be put apart seven days: and whosoever toucheth her shall be unclean until the even." Here we see that not only was this woman viewed as unclean, but every person who came into contact with her was unclean as well. The Bible goes on to say:

> **And every thing that she lieth upon in her separation shall be unclean: every thing also that she sitteth upon shall be unclean.**
>
> **And whosoever toucheth her bed shall wash his clothes, and bathe himself in water, and be unclean until the even.**
>
> **And whosoever toucheth any thing that she sat upon shall wash his clothes, and bathe himself in water, and be unclean until the even.**
>
> **And if it be on her bed, or on any thing whereon she sitteth, when he toucheth it, he shall be unclean until the even.**
>
> **And if any man lie with her at all, and her flowers be upon him, he shall be unclean seven days; and all the bed whereon he lieth shall be unclean.**
>
> **— Leviticus 15:20-24**

Are you beginning to see the severity of what this lady was facing? Every place she sat and everything she touched became contaminated. Likewise, every person who came in contact with her and whatever she touched was also considered unclean. Undoubtedly, this woman was viewed as a plague by others. No one wanted to be around her, much less touch her. And this avoidance wasn't just for a handful of days during her menstrual cycle — it was for *twelve years*. Scripture goes on to say:

> **And if a woman have an issue of her blood many days out of the time of her separation, or if it run beyond the time of her separation; all the days of the issue of her uncleanness shall be as the days of her separation: she shall be unclean.**
>
> **Every bed whereon she lieth all the days of her issue shall be unto her as the bed of her separation: and whatsoever she sitteth upon shall be unclean, as the uncleanness of her separation.**
>
> **And whosoever toucheth those things shall be unclean, and shall wash his clothes, and bathe himself in water, and be unclean until the even.**
>
> **— Leviticus 15:25-27**

So, in addition to being sick, this woman was a social outcast. Think about it. She lived in a perpetual state of uncleanness. If she was married, her husband wouldn't have been able to touch her. Even sitting or lying next to her would have placed him in the category of unclean. He couldn't have used the same dishes she used or touch anything that she touched. Likewise, if she had children, she couldn't have touched them, and they couldn't touch her — for twelve years. So, not only was she physically drained from the constant blood loss, but she was also depleted from living in social isolation.

'The Things' This Woman Heard About Jesus Infused Her Heart With Hope

Making matters even worse, this woman "…had suffered many things of many physicians, and had spent all that she had, and was nothing bettered, but rather grew worse" (Mark 5:26). In Greek, the word "suffered" is *pathos*, which includes *mental or emotional suffering*. The word "of" is also significant. It is the Greek word *hupo*, and it means *under* or *under the care or oversight of*. Its use in the context of this passage means this woman had been to doctor after doctor and was subjected to one test and treatment after another, but nothing had worked.

At this point, she "had spent all that she had." The word "spent" — the Greek word *dapanao* — means *to squander* or *to spend with great effort*. In hopes of being cured, this woman had searched diligently for the right medical treatments and drained her bank accounts in the process, but instead of getting better, she got worse.

Oh, but "when she had heard of Jesus, [she] came in the press behind, and touched his garment" (Mark 5:27). What's interesting about this verse is that the translators left out two words from the original text — the Greek words *ta peri*, which mean "the things." When we factor in these words, we could translate the opening of this verse to say, "When she heard *the things* about Jesus…" or "When she heard *the things concerning* Jesus…" or "When she heard *the things revolving around* Jesus…." Although this woman had lived in isolation because of her condition, for some reason she was on the street the day Jesus was in town, and she heard about *the things* He was doing.

What might she have heard? Well, she probably heard someone scream out, "My eyes are open! I can see!" or "My ears are open! I can hear!"

or even, "My child is healed and standing on his own two feet again!" Testimony after exciting testimony likely pierced the air, infusing hope into the hearts of all the hearers — including this woman with the issue of blood. As she heard the things concerning Jesus, faith began to rise within. "For she said, If I may touch but his clothes, I shall be whole" (Mark 5:28).

Interestingly, the tense of the word "said" — the Greek word *elegen* — conveys ongoing action. Therefore, a better translation would be, "*She said and said and kept on saying*, 'If I can just reach out and find a way to touch His clothes, I shall be whole.'" Notice the word "whole." It is the Greek word *sodzo*, which we just saw in Mark 5:23 — the New Testament word for *salvation* that also includes physical healing and *wholeness throughout one's body*.

When She Touched Jesus, She Was Made 'Whole'

When this woman touched Jesus, "…Straightway the fountain of her blood was dried up; and she felt in her body that she was healed of that plague" (Mark 5:29). The severity of this woman's problem can be seen in the word "fountain." It is the Greek word *pege*, which describes *a fountain, a spring*, or *a rushing fountain*. Clearly, her bleeding was major, not minor. Nevertheless, when she touched Jesus' clothes, she was "healed." In this verse, "healed" is the Greek word *iaomai*, which means *cured* or *doctored*. When she touched Jesus, the Great Physician, she was *progressively healed* of what the Bible calls her "plague."

The word "plague" in Mark 5:29 is really a poor translation. In Greek, it is the word *mastigos*, which is a term borrowed from the world of torture that denoted *the act of recurrently beating a prisoner or victim*. Once a person's wounds had mended, the torturers brought him back to the whipping post, where he was struck again and again and again. Such beatings were sporadic but constant, and although they were not usually serious enough to kill, it kept a victim in constant pain and misery.

In the case of the woman with the issue of blood, the word "plague" (*mastigos*) denotes *torment and abuse that caused great suffering and prolonged anguish*. Although the hemorrhaging didn't kill her, it was a recurring sickness or physical affliction that kept her in a protracted, repeated state of suffering. Other examples of *mastigos* would be migraine headaches, allergy attacks, and arthritis. A person who suffers with one of these issues may be fine for a while, and then suddenly it strikes them. Miraculously, Jesus healed this woman of her plague!

The Bible goes on to say, "And Jesus, immediately knowing in himself that virtue had gone out of him, turned him about in the press, and said, Who touched my clothes?" (Mark 5:30). The word "knowing" here is the Greek word *epiginosko*, which describes *expertise* or *professional knowledge*. Jesus was so in tune with the anointing of the Holy Spirit operating in His life that when virtue flowed out of Him, He was aware of it.

This brings us to the word "virtue," the wonderful Greek word *dunamis*. It describes *explosive, superhuman power that comes with enormous energy and produces phenomenal, extraordinary, and unparalleled results*. Moreover, it depicts "mighty deeds" that are impressive, incomparable, and beyond human ability to perform. Hence, Jesus' "virtue" was *the miraculous power* or *the miraculous manifestations* that flowed in and through His life.

Flabbergasted by Jesus' question, "…His disciples said unto him, Thou seest the multitude thronging thee, and sayest thou, Who touched me? And he looked round about to see her that had done this thing. But the woman fearing and trembling, knowing what was done in her, came and fell down before him, and told him all the truth" (Mark 5:31-33). The reason the woman was trembling and afraid was because as she came through the crowd to touch Jesus, she had touched many others, and technically she had made them unclean.

Would the people stone her for touching them as the law allowed? She didn't know, so she fell down at Jesus' feet only to hear Him say, "…Daughter, thy faith hath made thee whole; go in peace, and be whole of thy plague" (Mark 4:34). The word "whole" — which appears twice — is again the Greek word *sodzo*, and in addition to eternal salvation, it speaks of *wholeness in every part of life; a touch of salvation that brings delivering and healing power that results in wholeness*. This woman received wholeness in her body after being touched by Jesus' *dunamis* power!

'Stop Fearing and Be Believing'

Now, all this time Jairus, the leader of the synagogue, was alongside Jesus, desperately trying to get Him to his dying daughter. The Bible says, "While he [Jesus] yet spake, there came from the ruler of the synagogue's house certain which said, Thy daughter is dead: why troublest thou the Master any further? As soon as Jesus heard the word that was spoken, he

saith unto the ruler of the synagogue, Be not afraid, only believe"
(Mark 5:35,36).

When Jesus said, "Be not afraid, only believe," it was the equivalent of
Him saying, "Do not give into fear, but I charge you to only believe." In a
more roundabout way, Jesus was telling Jairus, "Stop fearing; be believing."

Scripture goes on to say, "And he [Jesus] suffered no man to follow him,
save Peter, and James, and John the brother of James. And he cometh to
the house of the ruler of the synagogue, and seeth the tumult, and them
that wept and wailed greatly. And when he was come in, he saith unto
them, Why make ye this ado, and weep? the damsel is not dead, but
sleepeth" (Mark 5:37-39).

The "tumult" Jesus saw in the house is the Greek word *thorubos*, and it
describes *a commotion and noise*. During that time, it was common to hire
flute players and others who performed public lamentations, so the haunting sound of the flute became synonymous with death and mourning.
When Jesus heard all the professional singers and musicians mourning
the loss of Jairus' daughter, He said, "Why make ye this ado, and weep?"
(Mark 5:39).

Interestingly, the word "ado" is the same Greek word for "tumult — the
word *thorubos*. "Why make all this commotion and noise?" Jesus asked.
"The damsel is not dead, but sleepeth" (Mark 5:39). Jesus knew she was
physically dead, but it was no harder for Him to raise someone from the
dead than it was to rouse someone from a nap. This was Jesus' way of saying, "Hey, death is not a problem or challenge for Me. I'm going to wake
this girl up from death just as I would wake somebody up from a nap."

At this, the Bible says, "…They laughed him to scorn…" (Mark 5:40). The
phrase "laughed…to scorn" is a translation of the Greek word *katagelao*,
which means *laughed, mocked*, or *ridiculed*. Amidst their laughter and ridicule
Jesus "put them all out" (Mark 5:40). What's interesting is that this phrase,
"put them all out," is a translation of the Greek word *ekballo* — the same
word translated "cast out," as in *cast out devils*. It means Jesus *threw out* or
forcefully evicted the mockers.

With the naysayers out of the room, Scripture says, "…He taketh the
father and the mother of the damsel, and them that were with him, and
entereth in where the damsel was lying. And he took the damsel by the
hand, and said unto her, Talitha cumi; which is, being interpreted, Damsel,

I say unto thee, arise. And straightway the damsel arose, and walked; for she was of the age of twelve years. And they were astonished with a great astonishment" (Mark 5:40-42). Through faith, Jairus' daughter received the healing Jairus longed for her to have.

In our final lesson, we will learn about the importance and power of the laying on of hands and what can happen when we reach out in faith to release God's healing to others.

STUDY QUESTIONS

**Study to shew thyself approved unto God, a workman that
needeth not to be ashamed, rightly dividing the word of truth.
— 2 Timothy 2:15**

1. The stories of Jairus seeking healing for his daughter and the woman with the issue of blood are quite moving. What new insights is the Holy Spirit showing you from their stirring testimonies?
2. Thinking about Jairus' position and the risk he was taking by going to Jesus, what trait did he have to have in order to make that choice? (*See* James 4:6 and First Peter 5:5.)
3. You may have heard of the woman with the issue of blood coming to Jesus for healing, but did you realize the scope of all the exhausting challenges she was facing? How do you think you would have responded to living is a perpetual state of uncleanness and isolation? How does this lesson expand your understanding of all that she was going through — and help you see your challenges in a different light?

PRACTICAL APPLICATION

**But be ye doers of the word, and not hearers only,
deceiving your own selves.
—James 1:22**

1. Remember how Jesus evicted the people who were laughing at and ridiculing Him when He went to raise Jairus' daughter? What does this tell you about the atmosphere necessary for healing to occur? Is there any "commotion" or negative "noise" you need to eliminate from your life that is hindering God's healing power? If so, what — or who — is it that you need to "put out"?

2.   Like the woman with the issue of blood, we all have some kind of
     pain (whether physical, mental, or emotional) that has caused us to
     feel ashamed, isolated, and an outcast. What have you been dealing
     with in your life that has left you feeling unclean and untouchable?
     Take time to reach out and touch God in prayer. Pour out your heart
     to Him and ask Him to increase your faith and to release His *sodzo*
     kind of healing that brings wholeness to every area of your life.

TOPIC

Healing Is in Your Hands

SCRIPTURES

1.   **Hebrews 13:8** — Jesus Christ the same yesterday, and to day, and for
     ever.

2.   **Acts 1:8** — But ye shall receive power, after that the Holy Ghost is
     come upon you....

3.   **Mark 16:17,18** — And these signs shall follow them that believe; In
     my name shall they cast out devils; they shall speak with new tongues;
     they shall take up serpents; and if they drink any deadly thing, it shall
     not hurt them; they shall lay hands on the sick, and they shall recover.

4.   **Mark 16:19,20** — So then after the Lord had spoken unto them, he
     was received up into heaven, and sat on the right hand of God. And
     they went forth, and preached every where, the Lord working with
     them, and confirming the word with signs following. Amen.

5.   **Hebrews 6:1,2** — Therefore leaving the principles of the doctrine of
     Christ, let us go on unto perfection; not laying again the foundation
     of repentance from dead works, and of faith toward God, of the doc-
     trine of baptisms, and of laying on of hands, and of resurrection of the
     dead, and of eternal judgment.

GREEK WORDS

1. "power" — **δύναμις** (*dunamis*): explosive power; a force of nature, like an earthquake, hurricane, or tornado; the full might of the advancing Roman army

2. "signs" — **σημεῖον** (*semeion*): the signature or seal applied to a document to guarantee its authenticity

3. "follow" — **παρακολουθέω** (*parakoloutheo*): a compound of **παρα** (*para*) and **ἀκολουθέω** (*akoloutheo*); the preposition **παρα** (*para*) means alongside, to be near, or to be in close proximity; the word **ἀκολουθέω** (*akoloutheo*) means to follow or to go somewhere with a person, as to accompany him on a trip; when compounded, as in this verse, the new word means to tirelessly accompany someone, to constantly be at the side of an individual, to always be in close proximity with a person, like a faithful companion who is always at one's side

4. "cast out" — **ἐκβάλλω** (*ekballo*): a compound of **ἐκ** (*ek*) and **βάλλω** (*ballo*); **ἐκ** (*ek*) means out, and **βάλλω** (*ballo*) means to throw; compounded, the new word means to throw out, as to evict someone from a place; to drive out; to expel; historically used to describe a nation that forcibly removed its enemies from its borders

5. "devils" — **δαιμόνιον** (*daimonion*): evil spirits; demons; devils; the ancient world generally believed demons thickly populated the lower regions of the air and that spirits were the primary cause of disasters and suffering in the earth; this word could depict a person deemed insane; in both secular and New Testament writings, it depicted those possessed with evil spirits who suffered spirit-inflicted mental or physical infirmities

6. "lay hands" — **ἐπιτίθημι** (*epitithemi*): a compound of the words **ἐπι** (*epi*) and **τίθημι** (*tithemi*); **ἐπι** (*epi*) means upon, and **τίθημι** (*tithemi*) means to place; when compounded, **ἐπιτίθημι** (*epitithemi*) means to place upon or to lay upon

7. "sick" — **ἄρρωστος** (*arrostos*): from the word **ῥώννυμι** (*rhunnumi*), which means to be well, strong, in good health, or possess a strong physical condition; when an "a" is placed in front of this word, it reverses the condition, and instead, the new word means to be in bad health or to possess a weak and broken condition; the image of a person so weak and sick that he has become critically ill; an invalid

8. "they shall" — ἔχω (*echo*): to have or to possess; the tense that is used in this verse doesn't picture something instantaneous; rather, it refers to something that occurs progressively

9. "recover" — καλῶς (*kalos*): to be well; to be healthy; to be in good shape

SYNOPSIS

The laying on of hands is one of the fundamental doctrines of the New Testament Church. The writer of Hebrews makes this clear in his letter, citing six basic teachings of the Christian faith, including: repentance from dead works, faith toward God, the doctrine of baptisms, laying on of hands, the resurrection of the dead, and eternal judgment (*see* Hebrews 6:1,2). Amazingly, right in the middle of these major doctrines is the doctrine of the laying on of hands. That shows just how important it is in God's eyes for us to understand what it means.

Look at your hands. They are one of the most amazing parts of your body! When God created you, He placed nearly 5 million touch receptors in you, and more than one-third of them are in your hands! Is it any wonder that God instructs us to lay hands on the sick so they will recover?

Remember, "Jesus Christ [is] the same yesterday, and to day, and for ever" (Hebrews 13:8). He used His hands to release healing into people's lives then, and He's still releasing healing into people's lives now — but He's doing it through *our* hands. We are the Body of Christ (*see* 1 Corinthians 12:27), and what Jesus does today He does through us by His Spirit. When our natural design combines with His supernatural power, extraordinary things are bound to happen!

The emphasis of this lesson:

When you believe, Jesus promised that supernatural signs will accompany you like traveling companions! Casting out evil spirits and seeing the sick healed when you lay hands on them are two signs you will see when you believe and pray in faith.

God Promised You POWER

Just before ascending into Heaven to take His seat at the right hand of the Father, Jesus told His followers not to leave Jerusalem but to wait for the promise of the Father (*see* Luke 24:49). He said, "But ye shall receive power, after that the Holy Ghost is come upon you…" (Acts 1:8). The word "power" here is the Greek word *dunamis*, and it describes *explosive power*. It is the same word the Greeks and Romans used to depict *a force of nature*, like *an earthquake*, *a hurricane*, or *a tornado*. Moreover, it was also the term used to describe *the full might of the advancing Roman army*.

What this means is that when we're filled with the Holy Spirit's power (*dunamis*), we become like *a spiritual force of nature* with the power to shake things up and blow things out of the way. His dynamic presence living within us is like the full might of an advancing army that takes enemy territory. If you are baptized in the Holy Spirit, His explosive, *dunamis* power is in you to be Christ's witness and do what you could never do on your own.

Jesus Promised You SIGNS

Along with the promise of God's power, Jesus promised His devoted followers that they would see specific supernatural *signs*. We read this declaration in Mark 16:17 and 18:

> **And these signs shall follow them that believe; In my name shall they cast out devils; they shall speak with new tongues; they shall take up serpents; and if they drink any deadly thing, it shall not hurt them; they shall lay hands on the sick, and they shall recover.**

The word "signs" in verse 17 is very important. It is the Greek word *semeion*, which was *the signature or seal applied to a document to guarantee its authenticity*. Jesus' promise of divine signs following those who believe is His promise of God's signature on your life and on the message of truth that you're sharing. When you go with the Gospel, God stands ready to place His signature on you and your efforts, and His signature will be signs and wonders! Supernatural manifestations will be the evidence that God has sent you and you're speaking His Word.

The second word to pay attention to is the word "follow." It is a translation of the Greek word *parakoloutheo*, which is a compound of *para* and *akoloutheo*. The preposition *para* means *alongside, to be near,* or *to be in close proximity*, and the word *akoloutheo* means *to follow* or *to go somewhere with a person*, as to accompany him on a trip. When compounded, as in this verse, the new word *parakoloutheo* means *to tirelessly accompany someone, to constantly be at the side of an individual,* or *to always be in close proximity with a person,* like a faithful companion who is always at one's side.

When you believe, Jesus promised that supernatural signs would follow you! In other words, these signs will be your traveling companions. Everywhere you go, they are to be constantly at your side because God promised that His signature of divine signs will tirelessly accompany those who believe.

Now, there's one stipulation: Jesus said, "And these signs shall follow *them that believe…*" (Mark 16:17). When you read this in the original Greek text, it says, "And these signs shall follow them that *are believing….*" The signature of God's signs doesn't follow them that *once believed.* Signs constantly accompany those who *are believing,* which means they are consistently engaging their faith looking for and trusting God to see supernatural signs *right now.*

Taking into account the original Greek meaning, here is the *Renner Interpretive Version* (*RIV*) of Mark 16:17:

> **These signs shall follow those who have engaged their faith and are believing….**

Those who see the greatest number of supernatural signs are those who consistently engage their faith and are believing to see them. In the program, Rick shared how his wife, Denise, is one of those people. Every day, everywhere she goes, she believes she is going to see manifestations of God's power show up to set people free and transform their lives — and she sees it. If you want to see supernatural signs and wonders in the lives of people around you, begin believing for them every day. Fill your mind and heart with God's Word and believe in faith to see God's signs manifest in people's lives.

You Can Cast Out Devils

Looking again at Mark 16:17, Jesus said, "And these signs shall follow them that believe; In my name shall they cast out devils…." Now, you may read this and think, *What does casting out demons have to do with healing?* The answer is, more than you think. All throughout the New Testament, we see that when Jesus brought healing to people, He often did it by casting out an evil or unclean spirit. To continue that same ministry, He has given us the same authority to cast out devils in His Name!

In Greek, the words "cast out" are a translation of the work *ekballo*, a compound of the words *ek* and *ballo*. The word *ek* means *out*, and *ballo* means *to throw*. When we compound these words to form *ekballo*, it means *to throw out*, as *to evict someone from a place*. It carries the idea of *driving out* or *expelling*. Historically, the word *ekballo* was also used to describe a nation that forcibly removed its enemies from its borders.

Spiritually speaking, if the enemy has invaded someone and that person is now under the influence of demons — or is *demonized* — those evil spirits are occupying territory that doesn't belong to them. As a believer, if you will engage your faith, you have the right to evict, expel, and drive them out. Now to do so, you will need to be very determined, which is inherently communicated in the word *ekballo*. But if you're persistent and demand the devils to leave, they will leave.

This brings us to the word "devils," which is the Greek word *daimonion*. It describes *evil spirits*, *demons*, or *devils*. As we've previously noted, the ancient world generally believed demons thickly populated the lower regions of the air and that spirits were the primary cause of disasters and suffering in the earth. This word *daimonion* could also depict *a person deemed insane*. In both secular and New Testament writings, it depicted those possessed with evil spirits who suffered spirit-inflicted mental or physical infirmities.

Again, Jesus dealt with demons all the time. Although people today don't talk about demons much, they're still here — they haven't evaporated. Our job is to understand how they operate and recognize when they're at work in someone's life. Once demonic activity is detected, we are to stand in our Christ-given authority and forcefully evict them from the person in the name of Jesus.

You Can Lay Hands on the Sick and They Will Recover!

Along with casting out devils and speaking in new tongues, Jesus said we will "…lay hands on the sick, and they shall recover" (Mark 16:18). Notice the words "they shall lay hands on." In Greek, "lay hands" is a translation of the word *epitithemi*, a compound of the words *epi* and *tithemi*. The word *epi* means *upon*, and *tithemi* means *to place*. When compounded, *epitithemi* means *to place upon* or *to lay upon*. Jesus said, if we are believing for healing, and we place our hands upon someone who is sick, they shall recover.

A careful study of Scripture reveals that people's hands always represented the conduit through which the power of God flowed. Remember when Jacob blessed Joseph's sons Ephraim and Manasseh? He spoke words of blessing while laying his hands on their heads (*see* Genesis 48:13-20). How about Moses? When his ministry had come to an end, Moses laid his hands on Joshua and imparted to him the Lord's mantle of leadership (*see* Deuteronomy 34:9). This same pattern continues right into the New Testament where we see Jesus laying hands on the sick to release healing and the apostles laying hands on people to receive the Holy Spirit (*see* Acts 8:18).

Again, our hands are the pipeline through which God's power and anointing flow. That includes YOUR hands. Jesus said if you will believe, in His Name you will lay YOUR hands on the sick and they shall recover. The word "sick" in Mark 16:18 is the Greek word *arrostos*, which is from the word *rhunnumi*, which means *to be well, strong, in good health*, or *possess a strong physical condition*. When an "a" is placed in front of the word *rhunnumi*, forming the word *arrostos*, it reverses the condition. Instead of good health and a strong physical condition, the new word *arrostos* means *to be in bad health* or *to possess a weak and broken condition*. It is the image of a person so weak and sick that he has become critically ill. This word can also describe *an invalid* or *someone who is bedfast* or even *comatose*.

As severe as all these conditions are, none are a match for the mighty authority of Jesus! If we'll lay our hands on anyone dealing with these sicknesses, Jesus said *they shall recover*. The words "they shall" is a form of the Greek word *echo*, which means *to have* or *to possess*. The tense used in this verse doesn't picture something instantaneous; rather, it refers *to something that occurs progressively over time*. So even though immediate restoration may not occur, we are still to lay hands on the sick and pro-claim their healing. The moment we do, God's power will be released to begin working in that person to reverse their condition.

Jesus said His power will flow through your hands, and those that are sick will *recover*. This word "recover" is the Greek word *kalos*, and it means *to be well, to be healthy*, or *to be in good shape*. Taking into account the original Greek meaning, here is the *Renner Interpretive Version* (*RIV*) of the latter part of Mark 16:18:

> …**They shall progressively feel themselves getting better and better, until finally they are well and healthy.**

God Will Confirm His Word
With Supernatural Signs

The Bible goes on to say, "So then after the Lord had spoken unto them, he was received up into heaven, and sat on the right hand of God. And they went forth, and preached every where, the Lord working with them, and confirming the word with signs following. Amen" (Mark 16:19,20).

Just as the Lord went with the disciples and worked with them in partnership, He will go with you and work side-by-side with you too. Remember, "Jesus Christ is the same yesterday, today, and forever" (Hebrews 13:8 *NKJV*). If He confirmed the Word they spoke with signs and wonders, He will confirm what you speak with signs and wonders as well. If you are believing for them, supernatural signs will be your constant companions everywhere you go.

Friend, it's time to engage your faith and be believing for big things to happen! When you walk out of your house every day, be ready to pray — and believe for people to be healed and set free from the power of the enemy. Get your hands out of your pockets and begin to place them on people who want to be healed. This is what it means to *engage your faith*, and this is how God's healing power is released. If you don't see instantaneous results, be at peace and trust that God is working, even if you can't see it.

Jesus said the sick will progressively recover if you will lay hands on them. Know that the moment you lay hands on the sick and pray in faith for them to be healed, God's healing power will begin to work, and from that time forward, they will begin to get better and better and better until they feel well and in full health again.

STUDY QUESTIONS

> **Study to shew thyself approved unto God, a workman that**
> **needeth not to be ashamed, rightly dividing the word of truth.**
> **— 2 Timothy 2:15**

1. As a believer, if you will engage your faith, you have the right to evict, expel, and drive out evil spirits that are harassing and depressing people. What kind of power has Jesus provided you through the finished work of the Cross? Study and commit to memory these amazing promises from His Word:

- Luke 9:1,2 and 10:19

- Second Corinthians 10:3,4

- Colossians 2:15

- Revelation 12:11

2. Jesus' promise of the Holy Spirit's power was for all His disciples —
    including you! Acts 2:39 (*NLT*) says the baptism in the Holy Spirit
    is for "…all who have been called by the Lord our God." Have you
    experienced this supernatural empowerment of the Holy Spirit? If so,
    are you praying daily in the special prayer language He has given you?
    According to First Corinthians 14:4 and Jude 20, what can you expect
    to happen when you "pray in the Spirit"?

3. If you haven't received the baptism in the Holy Spirit but would like
    to, take time to reflect on and do what Jesus said in Luke 11:9-13. As
    you are *ever-filled* with the Holy Spirit (*see* Ephesians 5:18), the signs
    Jesus promised will begin to happen more and more in and through
    your life!

PRACTICAL APPLICATION

**But be ye doers of the word, and not hearers only,
deceiving your own selves.**
—James 1:22

1. Your hands are the pipeline through which God's power and anoint-
    ing flow. Jesus said if you will believe, in His Name you will lay your
    hands on the sick and they shall recover. Do you believe what Jesus
    said? If not, pray and ask the Lord, *"What is keeping me from believing
    this truth that You spoke?"* Surrender to Him any fears or doubts He
    shows you and ask Him for the grace to believe Him for big things to
    take place through your hands.

2. Remember, God's signs don't follow them that *once believed*. His signs
    constantly accompany those who *are believing*. What can you do to
    more consistently engage your faith? Take a few moments to pray,
    *"Holy Spirit, how can I continue to increase my faith to believe You will do
    great things in and through me? What do I need to eliminate from my life
    that is causing me to doubt You, and what practice(s) can I add to increase
    my trust in You to see supernatural signs?"*

3. Friend, what do you need Jesus to do in your life? What kind of
    healing and restoration do you need? How about your family and your
    loved ones? God wants you to bring all these specific needs to Him in
    prayer (*see* Hebrews 4:16). He will provide for your needs and never
    leave you without support (*see* Hebrews 13:5). Jesus said if you will
    ask for *anything* in His Name, the Father in Heaven will do it, and He
    will receive glory (*see* John 14:13,14; 15:16; 16:23,24).

CLAIM YOUR FREE RESOURCE!

As a way of introducing you further to the teaching ministry of Rick Renner, we would like to send you FREE of charge his teaching, "How To Receive a Miraculous Touch From God" on CD or USB format.

In His earthly ministry, Jesus commonly healed *all* who were sick of *all* their diseases. In this profound message, learn about the manifold dimensions of Christ's wisdom, goodness, power, and love toward all humanity who came to Him in faith with their needs.

☑ **YES, I want to receive Rick Renner's monthly teaching letter!**

Simply scan the QR code to claim this resource or go to: **renner.org/claim-your-free-offer**

WITH US!

 renner.org

 facebook.com/rickrenner • facebook.com/rennerdenise

 youtube.com/rennerministries • youtube.com/deniserenner

 instagram.com/rickrenner • instagram.com/rennerministries_
instagram.com/rennerdenise